# All you need to know about Romania

Copyright © 2024 Jonas Hoffmann-Schmidt. Translation: Linda Amber Chambers.

All rights reserved. This book, including all its parts, is protected by copyright. Any use outside the narrow limits of copyright law is prohibited without the written consent of the author. This book has been created using artificial intelligence to provide unique and informative content.

Disclaimer: This book is for entertainment purposes only. The information, facts and views contained therein have been researched and compiled to the best of our knowledge and belief. Nevertheless, the author and the publisher assume no liability for the accuracy or completeness of the information. Readers should consult with professionals before making any decisions based on this information. Use of this book is the responsibility of the reader.

Introduction 6

Geography and landscape 9

History of Romania: From the Beginnings to the Present 12

The Dacians and the Roman era 15

The Middle Ages: Romania among principalities 17

Ottoman rule and the struggle for independence 20

Unification and modern Romania 23

Political system and current developments 27

Economy and trade 30

Society and demographic structure 33

Cultural diversity and ethnic groups 35

Religions in Romania 38

Languages and linguistics 40

Education System and Academic Institutions 42

Traditional festivals and customs 44

Modern Art und Kulturszene 46

Literature and important writers 48

Music and dance: folklore and contemporary trends 50

Architecture: From medieval fortresses to modern buildings 52

Culinary traditions and regional specialties 55

Romanian wines and the wine regions 57

The flora and fauna of Romania 60

Nature reserves and national parks 62

The Carpathians: Natural Wonders and Outdoor Adventure 64

The Danube and its importance for Romania 67

The Black Sea coast and its seaside resorts 69

Bucharest: capital between tradition and modernity 71

Timișoara: Capital of Culture and Multicultural Centre 74

Cluj-Napoca: university city and cultural hub 77

Sibiu: European Capital of Culture and Historical Heritage 80

Brasov: Gateway to the Carpathians and medieval flair 83

Iași: Cultural and intellectual stronghold of the East 86

Constanta: Port City and Ancient Past 89

The Moldavian Monasteries: UNESCO World Heritage Sites and Spiritual Oases 91

Transylvania: myths, legends and historical castles 93

Transylvania: Multicultural Diversity and Historical Traces 95

Bukovina: Artistic frescoes and traditional wooden churches 97

The Romanian language: origin, dialects and peculiarities 99

Travel tips and practical information 101

Famous people from Romania 104

Future prospects and challenges 106

Closing remarks 108

## Introduction

Romania, a fascinating country in southeastern Europe, characterized by a rich history, diverse culture and breathtaking nature. This introduction introduces you to the basics of this multifaceted country, which is often overshadowed by its Western European neighbours, but plays an independent and important role in Europe's history and present.

Geographically, Romania is located on the Balkan Peninsula and is surrounded by other countries on different sides: to the west and northwest of Hungary, to the north by Ukraine, to the east by Moldova and the Republic of Moldova, to the south by Bulgaria and to the southeast by Serbia. To the east, it is bordered by the Black Sea, which plays a significant role in the country's history and economic development.

The landscape of Romania is extremely diverse. To the north stretch the majestic Carpathian Mountains, one of the last untouched mountain regions in Europe, which is not only a paradise for nature lovers and hikers, but also home to a rich flora and fauna. The Southern Carpathians, Eastern Carpathians and Western Carpathians offer a variety of outdoor activities, from skiing in winter to hiking in summer.

Along the Danube stretches the fertile lowlands, which are traditionally used for agriculture and play an important role in the country's economic development. The Black Sea coast in the east offers not only miles of sandy beaches, but also historic towns and seaside resorts that attract tourists from all over Europe in the summer.

The history of Romania dates back thousands of years and is closely linked to the history of the peoples and empires that have passed through the country. The first known settlements emerged as early as the Paleolithic Age, and over the centuries different cultures and civilizations have shaped the country. The Dacians, a long-established population group conquered by the Romans in the first century BC, left significant archaeological traces, including the famous stone colossi of Sarmizegetusa Regia.

In the Middle Ages, the territory of Romania was divided into several principalities, which were created in the 14th and 15th centuries. The Ottomans conquered parts of the country in the 15th century and ruled the region until the end of the 19th century, while other areas were under Hungarian and Austrian rule. In the 19th century, a national movement emerged, which led to the unification of the Romanian principalities and finally led to the formation of the modern Romanian state in 1918.

Romania's cultural diversity is reflected in its traditions, customs, art forms, and architectural styles. Romanian folklore, rich in myths, legends and music, has a firm place in the national consciousness. Traditional dances such as the "hora" and musical instruments such as the pan flute are symbols of national identity.

The language of Romania, Romanian, belongs to the Eastern Romance languages and has a rich literary tradition. It is closely related to Italian, Spanish and French and has adopted many words from Latin. The language reflects the cultural diversity and historical influences that have shaped the country.

In the next chapters, we will dive deep into the different aspects of Romania, from its unique nature, to its historic cities and architectural treasures, to its modern society and economic development. Immerse yourself in this fascinating country and discover the treasures that Romania has to offer.

## Geography and landscape

Romania, a country in southeastern Europe, covers an area of about 238,397 square kilometers, making it one of the larger countries in the region. It is largely located on the Balkan Peninsula and borders Hungary to the west, Ukraine to the north, Moldova and the Black Sea to the east, Bulgaria and Serbia to the south. Its location at the crossroads of several geopolitical and cultural spheres of influence has had a strong impact on the country's history and development.

Romania's geographical landscape is extremely diverse, ranging from the majestic Carpathian Mountains in the north and west to the fertile lowlands along the Danube River in the south. The Carpathian Mountains, which crisscross the country from northwest to southeast, are one of Romania's most distinctive geographical features. They are divided into the Western Carpathians (Apuseni Mountains), the Southern Carpathians (Transylvanian Alps) and the Eastern Carpathians (Moldavian Carpathians), which together form a variety of mountain landscapes, valleys, gorges and peaks. The highest peak in Romania, Moldoveanu, rises 2,544 meters above sea level and is located in the Southern Carpathians.

The Carpathians are known not only for their scenic beauty, but also for their rich biodiversity. They are home to a variety of plant and animal species, including brown bears, lynxes, wolves, and rare bird species. National parks such as Retezat National Park and Rodna National Park provide protection for these ecosystems and attract nature enthusiasts and hikers from all over the world.

In the south and east of Romania, the vast lowlands stretch along the Danube, which is considered one of the most fertile regions in the country. This region is traditionally the center of Romanian agriculture and is known for the cultivation of cereals, sunflowers, grapes and fruit trees. The Danube itself plays a crucial role in the country's transportation and trade history, while also being an important waterway for transporting goods to Western and Eastern Europe.

The Black Sea coast stretches for about 245 kilometers and offers sandy beaches as well as historic towns and seaside resorts such as Constanta and Mamaia. The Black Sea plays an important role in tourism and fishing, providing a spectacular backdrop for visitors and locals alike.

In addition to the main landscape features, there are many other natural attractions in Romania, including caves such as the Scarisoara Ice Cave and the Pestera Ursilor, as well as gorges such as the Bicaz Gorge, which are popular destinations for adventure seekers and nature lovers.

Romania's geographical diversity and beauty make it a unique destination that has a lot to offer not only in terms of landscape, but also culturally and historically. In the following chapters, we will delve deeper into the history, culture, cities and other facets of this fascinating country.

# History of Romania: From the Beginnings to the Present

The history of Romania is deeply interwoven with the currents and influences of the peoples and empires that have crossed and shaped the area for thousands of years. The beginnings date back to prehistoric times, when the area was settled by various cultures, including the Neolithic culture, which introduced the first sedentary way of life and agricultural practices. Traces of this early settlement can be found in archaeological finds such as the clay figurines of Cucuteni-Trypillia, which are dated between 4500 and 2500 BC.

In the Iron Age and ancient times, the area of present-day Romania was settled by the Dacians, a Thracian people known for their mining skills and warfare. The Dacians repeatedly resisted the conquest attempts of the Romans until the area became part of the Roman Empire under Emperor Trajan in 106 AD. This period not only shaped the infrastructure and culture of the country, but also led to the development of the Romansh language and the Christianization of the population.

After the collapse of the Roman Empire and the migrations of the peoples, the area was crossed by the Ostrogoths, Huns, Avars and other groups before being integrated into the Byzantine Empire in the 9th century. In the 13th century, the country became a center of Orthodoxy and gained economic importance through trade with the Ottoman Empire.

Ottoman expansion in the 15th century led to a long struggle for independence and territorial integrity. While the southern and eastern parts of present-day Romania fell under Ottoman rule, the western and northern regions remained under Hungarian control. The three Romanian principalities of Moldavia, Wallachia and Transylvania were founded in the 14th and 15th centuries and played a decisive role in the preservation of national identity and culture.

The unification of the Romanian principalities in 1859 under Prince Alexandru Ioan Cuza laid the foundation for the modern Romanian nation. After the Russo-Ottoman War and the Congress of Berlin in 1878, Romania was recognized as an independent state and received royal status in 1881. During the First World War, Romania fought on the side of the Allies and gained territory and influence after the course of the war.

The interwar period was marked by political instability and economic challenges, which eventually led to the Communist Party under Gheorghe Gheorghiu-Dej coming to power in the late 1940s. The era of Nicolae Ceaușescu from the 1960s onwards was characterized by increasingly autocratic rule, economic mismanagement and oppression, culminating in the Romanian Revolution and the fall of the communist regime in 1989.

Since the revolution, Romania has undergone a transformation that includes the transition to a parliamentary democracy and a market economy. The country joined the European Union in 2004 and continues to strive for economic growth, social development and an increased role in the European and global community.

The history of Romania is a fascinating journey through the centuries, reflecting the heritage of different cultures and the perseverance of a people who fought against many challenges and political upheavals in order to preserve their identity and sovereignty.

## The Dacians and the Roman era

The Dacians were an ancient people who settled in the territories of present-day Romania and Moldova and developed a significant culture and civilization between the 3rd century BC and the 2nd century AD. They were known for their martial prowess and advanced metallurgical technology, especially in mining and the processing of gold and silver. The Dacians lived in well-organized settlements and built fortified towns and villages, some of which have been archaeologically studied, including Sarmizegetusa Regia and Costești.

In the 1st century BC, the Dacians came under pressure from the expanding Roman Republic and later the Roman Empire, which wanted to extend its control over the Balkan Peninsula. Under Emperor Trajan, the Romans began a campaign against the Dacians in 101 AD, which was fought in two major wars. The Dacians under their king Decebalus initially showed considerable resilience, but eventually they were defeated by the Romans in 106 AD.

The conquest of Dacia by the Romans led to the integration of the area into the Roman Empire and significant changes in the political, cultural and economic landscape. The Romans founded colonies, built cities and laid roads to develop and administer the region. The Romance culture, language and legal system were gradually adopted, which contributed to the emergence of the Romanian language and identity, which continue to this day.

An important testimony to the Roman presence in Dacia is the erection of Trajan's Column in Rome, which represents the Roman military campaigns against the Dacians. Roman settlements and villas, as well as thermal baths and amphitheatres, bear witness to the flourishing culture and prosperity that the Roman Empire brought to the region after the conquest. Roman rule lasted until the Romans' retreat from Dacia in 271 AD, when they were forced to tighten their borders and focus on defending the core empire.

The period of the Roman era in Dacia left a lasting impact on the region, especially through the adoption of technological, administrative and cultural achievements. The traces of the Roman occupation are clearly visible in the archaeological finds, the ruins of settlements and the historical records, which represent an important chapter in the history of Romania and laid the foundation for the development of an independent Romanian state.

# The Middle Ages: Romania among principalities

The Middle Ages mark an important period in Romania's history, marked by the formation and development of several independent principalities that shaped the political and cultural face of the country until its unification in the 19th century. The three main principalities were Moldavia, Wallachia, and Transylvania, each of which developed its own ruling structures, laws, and traditions while under various foreign influences.

Wallachia, also known as "Tara Românească" (the land of the Romanians), developed as one of the earliest principalities, with beginnings dating back to the 13th century. The rulers of Wallachia often fought for autonomy from Hungarian and Ottoman domination, while at the same time building relationships with other European powers. Well-known rulers such as Mircea the Elder and Vlad III Drăculea, also known as Vlad the Impaler, have become part of Wallachian history and mythology.

Moldavia, or "Țara Moldovei", also developed into an independent principality in the 14th century under the rule of Prince

Dragoș and his son Bogdan I. Moldavia experienced a prosperous period under Stephen the Great (Ștefan cel Mare), who ruled in the 15th century and was known for his victories against the Ottoman Empire and his promotion of art, literature and architecture. Moldavia remained an independent principality until its unification with Wallachia in 1859.

Transylvania, or "Transilvania", was a multi-ethnic principality that was under Hungarian and later Habsburg rule. It developed into a significant cultural and economic center with a variety of ethnic and religious groups, including Romanians, Hungarians, Germans (Transylvanian Saxons) and Roma. The region was known for its medieval cities such as Sibiu, Brasov and Cluj-Napoca, as well as for its fortresses and trade routes that made it a crossroads between East and West.

During the Middle Ages, Romanian principalities often had to contend with the challenges of Ottoman expansion, which led to tribute payments and occasional military conflicts. Nevertheless, the principalities managed to maintain their independence while maintaining an independent culture and identity that was shaped by Orthodox Christianity, local traditions and a rich oral tradition.

The political structures of the principalities were often characterized by feudalism and a strong tradition of rule, while cities and villages developed under the auspices of the local boyars and princes. Churches and monasteries played a central role in religious and social life, while art and architecture found expression in the form of Orthodox churches with painted facades and wooden monasteries.

The Middle Ages were a time of challenge and change for the Romanian principalities, which laid the foundations for modern Romania, both politically and culturally. The unity of the Romanian lands in the 19th century marked the end of the medieval era and the beginning of a new phase of national identity and state sovereignty.

## Ottoman rule and the struggle for independence

Ottoman rule over Romania began in the early 15th century and lasted until the late 19th century. It left a profound impact on the country's history, culture, and society, shaping its development over several centuries. After the Battle of Mohács in 1526, in which the Kingdom of Hungary was defeated by the Ottomans, the Kingdom of Hungary and thus the then Principality of Transylvania also came under Ottoman rule.

For the principalities of Wallachia and Moldavia, Ottoman rule meant a complex balance between autonomy and tribute payments to the Ottoman Empire. The Ottoman sultans regularly installed local princes known as hospodaries, and exercised direct control over foreign policy and taxation. The Ottoman presence led to an Islamization of some parts of the population, especially in the urban centers, while the Orthodox Church and local customs were largely preserved.

During Ottoman rule, the Romanian principalities of Wallachia and Moldavia experienced periods of relative calm and prosperity, but also periods of political intrigue and internal unrest. Ottoman interests in the region were strongly influenced by strategic considerations to defend against Austrian and Russian expansionist ambitions, which led to a complicated geopolitical situation.

In the 18th century, aspirations for independence began to stir in the Romanian principalities, driven by the nationalist movement and the ideals of the Enlightenment. The power of the Ottoman central government weakened, while local rulers such as Michael the Brave (Mihai Viteazul) tried to strengthen the independence of the Romanian lands and carry out territorial expansions against Ottoman and Habsburg powers.

The phase of the struggle for independence reached a climax in the 19th century, when the Romanian principalities sought the status of complete sovereignty under the leadership of Prince Alexandru Ioan Cuza and later under Prince Carol I. The Romanian Revolution of 1848 and support from other European powers, notably Russia, played a crucial role in the abolition of Ottoman suzerainty and the recognition of Romania's independence through the Treaty of Berlin in 1878.

The Ottoman rule and the struggle for independence left a legacy of political, cultural and religious diversity in Romania. The history of this era is marked by complex relations between the Romanian principalities and the Ottoman Empire, as well as by the search for national identity and self-determination, which continues to influence Romanian society and politics today.

# Unification and modern Romania

The unification of the Romanian principalities marked a decisive turning point in the history of Romania and laid the foundation for the emergence of the modern Romanian state in the 19th century. After centuries under Ottoman rule and a multitude of political and cultural challenges, the Romanian principalities of Moldavia and Wallachia strove for a common identity and national unity.

Efforts to unite were reinforced by the nationalist movement in the 19th century, which was supported by intellectuals, academics and political leaders who cherished the vision of a united Romanian state. The 1848 revolution in the principalities, which was part of the broader European revolutionary movement, demanded reforms and autonomy from Ottoman rule and reinforced demands for national unity.

The decisive steps towards unification were taken in the 1850s, when Prince Alexandru Ioan Cuza ruled both Wallachia and Moldavia, initiating reforms to modernize society and the economy. On January 24,

1859, Alexandru Ioan Cuza was elected ruler of both principalities, formally marking the union of the two regions under a common leadership.

However, the final unification of the principalities of Wallachia and Moldavia was not completed until 1862 by a formal acclamation of the respective noble assemblies, which confirmed Cuza as domnitor (prince) over both territories. This union was a significant step towards national unity and sovereignty, although the country remained under the nominal protection of the great powers, especially France and Great Britain.

The next milestone on the way to modern Romania was the election of Carol I of the House of Hohenzollern-Sigmaringen as Prince in 1866. Carol I carried out far-reaching reforms and strengthened the country's institutions, which led to the proclamation of Romania as a kingdom in 1881. Under his leadership and through skillful diplomatic maneuvers, Romania managed to achieve territorial expansions, including the recovery of southern Dobruja from Bulgaria after the Russo-Ottoman War of 1877-1878.

World War I brought significant losses and challenges to Romania, including the occupation of parts of the country by the Central Powers. After the war, however, the unification of Transylvania, which had previously been under Hungarian rule, with Romania was completed. This led to the territorial expansion and integration of other ethnic Romanian territories into the Romanian state.

The interwar period was marked by political instability and the rise of the authoritarian regime of King Carol II. After a short period of neutrality, Romania joined the Tripartite Pact in 1940, which led to territorial losses, including Bessarabia and northern Bukovina to the Soviet Union and parts of Transylvania to Hungary.

During World War II, Romania fought on the side of the Axis powers until a reversal of the alliances led to the Soviet occupation of the country by the Soviet Union in August 1944. This paved the way for the establishment of a communist government led by Gheorghe Gheorghiu-Dej, followed by Nicolae Ceaușescu in the 1960s.

The 1989 revolution ended the communist era in Romania and led to the restoration of democracy and the market economy. Romania joined the European Union in 2004 and has since made significant progress in areas such as economic development, infrastructure and social inclusion.

The unification of the Romanian principalities and the development into modern Romania reflect a long path of challenges, upheavals and achievements that have shaped the country's national identity and self-image. Today, Romania is a sovereign state on the international stage and continues to strive for a stable and prosperous future for its citizens.

# Political system and current developments

Romania's political system is characterised by a parliamentary democracy, which has been established since the revolution of 1989 after the fall of the communist regime. According to the 1991 Constitution, Romania is a republic in which the executive, legislative, and judicial branches are separated. The head of state is the president, who is elected every five years by direct elections. The president has powers set out in the constitution, including the appointment of the prime minister and the representation of the country at the international level.

The legislature consists of two chambers: the Senate and the Chamber of Deputies, which are collectively known as the Parliament. Members of Parliament are elected every four years and represent the interests of citizens in legislation and policy-making. Romania uses a mixed electoral system, which uses a combination of proportional representation and majority voting.

The prime minister is the head of the government and is appointed by the president after gaining the confidence of parliament. The government is responsible for the implementation of the laws and the administration of the country, including the areas of economy, education, health care, and foreign policy. Romania's political life is characterized by a variety of political parties, ranging from conservative to socialist ideologies.

In recent decades, Romania has experienced a number of political challenges and developments. Romania's accession to the European Union in 2007 was an important step that involved the country in the European integration process and promoted economic and political reforms. Nevertheless, corruption remains a prominent challenge in the political system, with progress being made in the fight against corruption and strengthening the rule of law.

Romania's relations with its neighbours and international partners are important for its security and economic development. Romania is a member of NATO and plays an active role in the Black Sea's regional security architecture. Diplomatic relations with countries in the EU and around the world are of strategic importance to promote common interests and address global challenges.

More recently, Romania has faced social tensions and political unrest, particularly in the context of reforms in the judiciary and public administration. The country's citizens have actively participated in political demonstrations and elections to make their voices heard and work towards changes in the political landscape.

Romania's political system and current developments reflect a country that is in a phase of transformation, while continuing to strengthen its democratic institutions and face the challenges of the global world. The country's future will depend largely on its ability to ensure political stability, drive reforms and effectively represent the needs of its citizens.

## Economy and trade

Romania's economy is one of the largest in Southeastern Europe and has developed significantly since the end of the communist regime in 1989. The country has a diverse economy characterized by industry, agriculture, services and, increasingly, the IT sector. After the transition to a market economy in the 1990s, Romania went through a phase of economic transformation and structural adjustment, which led to dynamic growth and the modernisation of the economic structure.

Industry is an important sector of the Romanian economy and includes areas such as mechanical engineering, automotive production, electronics, chemicals and textiles. Car manufacturers such as Dacia, a subsidiary of Renault, have made significant investments and contribute to the country's industrial production and export capacity. Romania is also a major producer of electronics and IT services, with cities such as Cluj-Napoca being known as technology hubs.

Agriculture continues to play an important role in the Romanian economy, especially in rural areas where traditional agricultural practices coexist with modern technologies. Romania is a major producer of corn, wheat, barley, sunflower, sugar beet, potatoes and grapes, which are grown both for domestic consumption and export. Livestock farming, especially pig and cattle farming, is also an important economic sector.

In the service sector, tourism, financial services, IT and telecommunications have developed into strong growth areas. The tourism sector benefits from the country's rich history and culture, as well as natural beauties such as the Carpathian Mountains and the Black Sea coast. Romania is a popular destination for cultural tourists visiting historic cities such as Bucharest, Sibiu and Brașov, as well as nature lovers enjoying the pristine landscapes of the Danube Delta and mountainous regions.

Romania's foreign trade has diversified considerably since joining the EU in 2007, with EU countries being its main trading partners. The main exports include machinery and equipment, electronics, motor vehicles, agricultural products, and textiles. Imports are concentrated in machinery and equipment, petroleum products, chemical products and electronic goods. Romania is part of the EU's internal market and benefits from free trade and investment within the Union.

However, Romania's economy faces challenges such as high unemployment in rural areas, inequalities in regional development, corruption and inefficient administration. The government has implemented reforms to improve the business climate, attract investment, and modernize infrastructure. Despite these challenges, Romania remains a country with significant economic potential, supported by its strategic location, natural resources and emerging workforce.

# Society and demographic structure

Romanian society is diverse and reflects the historical, cultural, and ethnic influences that have shaped the country. The population of Romania is about 19 million people and is ethnically heterogeneous, with the majority being of Romanian descent. However, there are significant minorities such as Hungary, Roma, Germans (Transylvanian Saxons), and other ethnic groups that contribute to the country's cultural diversity.

The demographic structure of Romania shows an aging population with an average median age of about 43 years. The birth rate is low and the population tends to decline, partly due to emigration and economic challenges. The urban areas, especially Bucharest and other larger cities, attract young people, while rural areas are affected by an aging population and a low birth rate.

Romanian society is strongly influenced by the Orthodox Church, which plays an important role in public life and traditional values. Religion is an integral part of cultural identity, although the country is also home to a variety of other religious groups and denominations.

In terms of education and health, Romania has made progress, although there are challenges such as an unequal distribution of resources between urban and rural areas. The education system includes free primary and secondary education, as well as universities and colleges that offer broad educational opportunities. Health care has improved, although the system faces challenges such as limited resources and unequal accessibility to health services.

Ethnic minorities, especially the Roma population, face social and economic challenges, including discrimination, poverty and lack of integration. The government has developed programs to promote the integration and support of minorities in order to promote equal opportunities and social justice.

Overall, Romanian society reflects a complex mix of tradition and modernity, with a population that strives to adapt to the challenges of the 21st century and promote sustainable development in all areas of social and economic life.

# Cultural diversity and ethnic groups

Romania is a country with a rich cultural diversity, made up of a variety of ethnic groups and historical influences. The Romanian population is largely ethnically Romanian, but there are significant minorities that enrich the social and cultural fabric of the country. One of the largest ethnic minorities are the Hungarians, who live mainly in the Transylvania region and have a significant cultural presence, including their own schools, media and cultural events.

The Roma population, also known as gypsies, is one of the largest minorities in Romania and one of the most marginalized groups. They make up about 3-5% of the total population and are historically present in rural areas as well as in urban settlements. Roma communities face challenges such as discrimination, social exclusion and economic disadvantage, despite efforts to integrate and promote their rights.

The German minority, known as the Transylvanian Saxons, has a long history in Romania, dating back to the Middle Ages. They are mainly concentrated in Transylvania and have made significant cultural and economic contributions, although their numbers have decreased significantly since the end of the communist regime, mainly due to emigration to Germany.

Other ethnic groups in Romania include Ukrainian, Serbian, Bulgarian and Turkish communities, which are mainly represented in the border regions of the country. These groups contribute to the diversity of languages, customs and traditions that enrich Romania's cultural heritage.

In terms of religious diversity, Romania is mainly Orthodox Christian, with the Romanian Orthodox Church being the dominant denomination. In addition to the Orthodox community, there are also important Roman Catholic, Greek Catholic, Protestant and other Christian communities. In addition, there is a Muslim minority, mainly in Dobruja, as well as small Jewish communities that are historically rooted in Romania.

Romania's cultural landscape is characterized by a variety of traditions, festivals, music, dance, and literature that reflect the national heritage. Traditional Romanian folk arts such as wood carving, pottery and embroidery have a long history and are appreciated by both locals and tourists.

Overall, the cultural diversity and coexistence of different ethnic groups in Romania reflects a rich and complex society that is proud of its cultural heritage while striving to promote the integration and rights of all citizens.

## Religions in Romania

The religious landscape of Romania is mainly characterized by the Romanian Orthodox Church, which is the largest religious denomination in the country. About 81% of the population belongs to the Romanian Orthodox Church, which is deeply rooted in the country's history and culture. The Romanian Orthodox Church follows the Eastern Church tradition and has an important role in public life, holidays and the traditional customs of Romanian society.

In addition to the Romanian Orthodox Church, there are a variety of other religious communities in Romania. The Roman Catholic Church is the second largest Christian denomination in the country and has historical roots in Transylvania as well as in other parts of Romania. The Greek Catholic Church, also known as Uniate or Romanian Greek Catholic Church, is a significant religious community that unites both the Orthodox tradition and Catholic doctrine.

Protestantism also has a significant following in Romania, especially among the Hungarian and German minorities in Transylvania. Protestant denominations include Lutherans, Reformed, Baptists, and other evangelical groups. These communities have historical roots in the

Reformation period and play an important role in the religious life of their communities. In addition, there is a Muslim minority in Romania, mainly in Dobruja in the south-east of the country. Romania's Muslim community includes various ethnic groups, including Turks, Tatars, and Roma, who practice Islam and maintain mosques and cultural institutions.

Judaism has a long history in Romania, although the Jewish population has declined sharply over the course of the 20th century due to migration. Historic Jewish communities, especially in cities such as Bucharest and Iași, have left their mark on Romanian culture and history, although today's Jewish community is smaller.

In addition to these main religions, there are smaller religious groups and denominations, including Jehovah's Witnesses, Mormons, and other Christian sects, as well as various new religious movements.

The Romanian constitution guarantees freedom of religion and separates church and state, although the Orthodox Church has historically held a privileged position. Religious holidays and traditions play an important role in Romania's cultural calendar, offering insight into the diversity and richness of religious beliefs and practices that shape the country's social fabric.

## Languages and linguistics

Romania's linguistic landscape is diverse and reflects the country's complex history and ethnic diversity. The official language is Romanian, which belongs to the eastern subgroup of the Romance languages and is closely related to Italian, Spanish, French and Portuguese. Romanian is spoken as a native language by about 85% of the population and is the most important language for public service, education and media in the country.

In addition to Romanian, Hungarian and German are the most important minority languages in Romania. Hungarian is mainly spoken by the Hungarian minority in Transylvania and has official status in the regions where Hungary is concentrated. Germans, known as Transylvanian Saxons, have historical roots in Transylvania and speak a dialect of German that is closely related to High German.

Romani, the language of the Roma community in Romania, is also present and spoken by part of the Roma population, although it is used more as a minority language in informal situations. Other languages spoken by ethnic minorities include Serbian, Ukrainian, Bulgarian, and Turkish, which are cultivated in their respective communities.

The Romanian language has evolved throughout history through various influences, including Latin (due to the Roman occupation), Slavic (through contacts with Slavic peoples), and Hungarian (through the rule of the Kingdom of Hungary over parts of the country). Modern Romanian also includes loanwords from other European languages, as well as from Turkish and Greek due to historical interactions with the Ottoman Empire and Byzantium.

Linguistically, Romanian shows phonetic and grammatical peculiarities compared to other Romance languages, especially in the stress and structure of nouns and verbs. There are various regional dialects within Romania that are shaped by geographical and historical factors, but Standard Romanian is based on the dialect of the region around Bucharest and is used nationwide in education and media.

Romania's language policy promotes multilingualism and the protection of minority languages, while Romanian is considered a single language and an instrument of national identity. Linguistic diversity and the richness of the Romanian language reflect the cultural dynamism of the country and contribute to the cultural identity and integration of the different ethnic groups.

# Education System and Academic Institutions

Romania's education system is characterised by a structure that integrates elements from both the communist era and the requirements of a modern, globalised society. The public education system is free and compulsory for children aged 6 to 16, consisting of primary and secondary school levels. Basic education has a strong focus on basic skills in literacy, mathematics and science, although the quality and resources of schools may vary depending on the region and financial support.

After compulsory schooling, pupils have the opportunity to attend secondary schools, which can be either general grammar schools or vocational schools. The general education high school prepares students for higher education and offers various academic profiles, including science, humanities, languages, and mathematics. Vocational schools offer practical training in various occupational fields to improve the employability of graduates.

Romania's higher education system includes universities, polytechnics, and other higher education institutions that offer a wide range of study programs in various disciplines. Universities are usually state or private and offer bachelor's, master's, and doctoral programs. The country's best-known universities are located in Bucharest, Cluj-Napoca, Iași, Timișoara, and other major cities, each with its own focus and research areas.

Higher education in Romania faces challenges such as limited financial resources, a lack of modern equipment and a sometimes inadequate link between higher education and the needs of the labour market. Nevertheless, Romanian universities have made progress in reaching international standards and providing a high-quality education that provides both theoretical knowledge and practical skills.

Research and development in Romania is supported by state and private investment, with universities, research institutes and companies collaborating on projects aimed at technological innovation, scientific discoveries and societal challenges. The country is striving to integrate into European research networks and to expand international cooperation in science and education.

Overall, Romania's education system plays a crucial role in developing human resources, fostering innovation and strengthening national competitiveness. Through continuous reforms and investments, Romania strives to improve the quality of education and promote equal opportunities for all citizens.

# Traditional festivals and customs

Romania is rich in traditional festivals and customs that are deeply rooted in the country's history and culture. These celebrations reflect the diversity of regional traditions and the connection to agricultural rhythms and religious holidays.

An important festival, for example, is Easter, which is celebrated as one of the most important religious events in the Orthodox calendar. The Easter celebrations in Romania are rich in symbolic rituals such as the dyeing of eggs in vivid colors and the traditional Easter feast, which consists of specialties such as lamb dishes and Easter bread.

Another notable celebration is the Romanian "Dragobete", a day of celebration similar to traditional Romanian Valentine's Day, often associated with the beginning of spring. It is an occasion to celebrate love and affection, often expressed through flowers and small gifts.

The Romanian "Martisor" is another traditional festival that marks the beginning of spring. On this day, small pins in red and white are worn, which are considered lucky charms and symbols of health and fertility.

Regional festivals such as the "Young Girls Festival" in Bucovina, the "Bear Dance" in Moldova and the "Haiducii Dance" in the mountains of the Carpathians offer insights into local traditions and folkloric customs, often associated with music, dance and handicrafts.

In autumn, Romania celebrates Thanksgiving, known as "Sânziene", which was originally a pagan ritual that was later incorporated into the Christian festival. It is a time of thanksgiving for the harvest yields and is often celebrated with songs, dances and special feasts.

The traditional Romanian wedding feast is also of great importance, with an abundance of ancient customs and rites symbolizing the union of the bride and groom. These include exchanging gifts, tying wreaths, and performing dance rituals that often last into the night.

The diversity and vibrancy of the traditional festivals and customs in Romania not only reflect the historical and cultural roots of the country, but also serve as a living reminder of the identity and cohesion of the communities in different regions of the country.

## Modern Art und Kulturszene

The modern art scene in Romania has undergone a remarkable development in recent decades, characterized by a diversity of artistic expressions and an increasing commitment on an international level. Bucharest, as the country's capital, functions as a center for contemporary art and is home to a variety of galleries, museums, and cultural institutions showcasing modern Romanian artists as well as international artists.

Romanian artists have achieved great success in various areas of contemporary art, including painting, sculpture, installations, photography, and new media. Her works often reflect social, political, and cultural issues, as well as personal experiences and identity. Many artists use traditional Romanian motifs and symbols and interpret them in a contemporary context.

In addition to Bucharest, other cities such as Cluj-Napoca, Timişoara, Iaşi, and Braşov also have an active art scene, fostered by art galleries, art festivals, and creative communities. These cities serve as platforms for young emerging artists as well as established names in the Romanian art scene, known for their diversity and innovation.

Cultural events and festivals play an important role in the promotion of modern art in Romania. The George Enescu Festival in Bucharest is one of the most prestigious music festivals in Europe and attracts artists and audiences from all over the world. The Transilvania International Film Festival (TIFF) in Cluj-Napoca is an important film event in the region and provides a platform for international and Romanian filmmakers.

The literary scene in Romania is also vibrant, with a rich tradition of writers and poets who have gained national and international recognition. Romanian authors such as Mircea Eliade, Emil Cioran, Herta Müller and Norman Manea have created important literary works that have been translated into many languages and enrich the country's cultural heritage.

Romania's cultural scene faces challenges such as limited financial resources, the need for infrastructure improvement, and the promotion of artistic education and development. Nevertheless, the country's modern art and culture has produced a dynamic and eclectic scene that reflects the creative energy and artistic expression of Romanian society.

## Literature and important writers

Romanian literature has a rich history that dates back to ancient times and is marked by various historical and cultural influences. An early work that had a significant influence on Romania's literary tradition is the "Codex Rohonczi", a medieval manuscript that contains Romanian and Hungarian texts and provides important cultural and historical information about the Transylvania region.

In the 19th century, Romanian literature experienced a heyday, with many writers dedicated themselves to promoting the Romanian language and identity. Mihai Eminescu is considered one of the most important poets of this period and is known for his lyrical works that express the beauty of Romanian landscapes and the longing for national freedom and identity.

Another important writer of the 19th century was Ion Creangă, whose works capture Romanian folk culture and oral storytelling tradition. His work "Amintiri din copilărie" (Memories from Childhood) is a classic of Romanian literature and describes rural life and customs of the time.

Romanian literature of the 20th century was shaped by various currents, including the avant-garde movement and existentialist philosophy. Eugen Ionescu, an important representative of the theatre of the absurd, came from Romania and his plays such as "The Bald Singer" and "The Rhinoceroses" are known worldwide.

In the field of prose, Mircea Eliade is one of the most influential Romanian writers of the 20th century, known for his works on religion, mythology and human existence. His novel "The Sons of the Earth" and his stories have gained international recognition and shape the understanding of spirituality and cultural history.

The Romanian Nobel Prize winner for literature Herta Müller is one of the country's most prominent contemporary writers, known for her poetic prose and unmistakable style. Her works often deal with topics such as dictatorship, oppression and exile, which she reflects on from personal experience as a German-born writer in Romania.

The Romanian literary landscape remains dynamic and diverse, with a new generation of writers grappling with current societal challenges and global issues. Authors such as Norman Manea, Mircea Cărtărescu and Ioan Petru Culianu champion the tradition of Romanian literature and contribute to the cultural diversity and identity of the country.

## Music and dance: folklore and contemporary trends

The Romanian musical tradition is rich and diverse, with a mix of folkloric roots and modern influences, encompassing a vibrant scene from folk music to contemporary genres. Folklore has a deep cultural value in Romania and reflects the traditional ways of life, customs and stories of the different regions of the country.

The musical traditions of Romania's various ethnic groups, including Romanians, Hungarians, Germans, Roma and others, have produced unique musical expressions. Romanian folk music is known for its variety of instruments such as the pan flute (nai), the violin (vioara cu goarnă), the cimbalom (cimpoi) and the bagpipes (tulnic), which are often played at traditional celebrations and events.

Each region of Romania has its own specific musical styles and dances. For example, the dance styles in Transylvania, Bukovina, Moldova and the Carpathians are different and reflect the historical and cultural differences of the communities living there. The "Hora" is a well-known Romanian round dance that is danced in various variations throughout Romania and is often accompanied by a lively musical accompaniment. In addition to traditional folk music, Romania has a vibrant contemporary music scene that spans a wide range of genres, including pop, rock, hip-hop, electronic music, and experimental music. Bucharest is the center of contemporary music production, home to numerous recording studios, concert halls, and music festivals that attract both local and international artists.

Romanian pop music has grown in popularity over the past few decades, with artists such as Inna, Alexandra Stan, and Voltaj enjoying international success. Rock music also has a loyal fan base in Romania, with bands such as Phoenix and Iris making significant contributions to the national music scene. Music festivals such as the Electric Castle Festival, the Untold Festival and the Jazz in the Park Festival in Cluj-Napoca have become significant events that attract thousands of music fans from all over the world. These festivals provide a platform for local and international artists to showcase their talents and celebrate the cultural diversity of Romania's music scene.

Overall, the Romanian musical landscape remains dynamic and creative, fusing traditional elements with modern influences to create a rich and diverse soundscape that reinforces the country's cultural heritage while exploring new artistic horizons.

# Architecture: From medieval fortresses to modern buildings

Romania's architecture is a fascinating reflection of its rich history and cultural diversity, which has been shaped over centuries. Starting with the medieval fortresses, which were often built on strategic hills to protect the country from invaders, there are numerous examples of such constructions throughout Romania. One of the most famous is the Suceava Fortress in Bukovina, built in the 14th century and considered one of the most important medieval fortresses in the country.

Another outstanding example of medieval architecture is the Church of Densus, a Romanesque church from the 13th century, considered the oldest stone church in Romania, with its massive stone walls and frescoes dating back to the 14th century.

Renaissance and Baroque architecture also left their mark on Romania, especially in the cities of Transylvania such as Cluj-Napoca and Sibiu, where magnificent town houses and churches in the Baroque style can be found. A notable example is the Brukenthal Palace Gallery in Sibiu, an 18th-century

Baroque masterpiece that now serves as a museum.

In the 19th and early 20th centuries, Romania experienced a building boom characterized by neoclassical and Art Nouveau architecture. Known as the "Little Paris of the East," Bucharest is rich in Art Nouveau buildings and elegant palaces that reflect the heyday of Romanian culture and society. The Athénée Palace Hilton Hotel and the Kretzulescu Palace are outstanding examples of this era.

Modernist architecture gained prominence after World War II, when Romania was under communist rule. Bucharest became an experimental field for socialist architecture and urban planning, with monumental structures such as the House of the People (now the Palace of Parliament), which is considered the second largest building in the world.

After the communist era, Romania has experienced a period of architectural renewal, with modern and contemporary architecture showing new developments in urban planning and design. Modern high-rise buildings and shopping malls in Bucharest, as well as renowned architects such as Anca Petrescu, have shaped the country's urban landscape, while restored historic buildings and monuments preserve the legacy of the past.

Overall, Romania's architecture reflects a fascinating mix of historical traditions and modern influences that have shaped the country's cultural and architectural development over the centuries.

## Culinary traditions and regional specialties

Romania's culinary traditions are characterized by a variety of flavors that reflect the country's history, geography and cultural influences. Romanian cuisine combines elements from Balkan, Eastern European, Turkish and Hungarian cuisine to create a unique gastronomic landscape.

One of the most famous specialties is "sarmale", a type of stuffed cabbage rolls stuffed with minced meat and rice and wrapped with sauerkraut or vine leaves. Often served on festive occasions such as weddings or Christmas, this dish symbolizes the hospitality and tradition in Romanian households.

Another traditional specialty is "Mămăligă", a cornmeal porridge prepared in a similar way to polenta and often served with cheese, cream or meat. Mămăligă is a staple in Romanian cuisine and is often eaten as an accompaniment to meat dishes such as "mititei" (spiced minced meat rolls) or "ciorbă" (a sour soup).

The "Țuică" is a traditional Romanian brandy distilled from plums or other fruits and consumed on many social occasions, especially in the countryside. It is a symbol of Romanian hospitality and is often distilled and drunk in small village inns or at family celebrations.

Romania's regional diversity is also reflected in its culinary traditions. In Bukovina, "Ciorbă de burtă", a sour soup with tripe, is a popular dish, while in Transylvania, dishes such as "Papanași", fried curd balls with sour cream and jam, are widespread.

The Danube Delta region is known for its fish dishes, including "Storioni" (sturgeon) and "Scrumbii" (herring), which are often served grilled or smoked. These dishes are an essential part of the diet of the people who live along the rivers and lakes of the delta.

Romanian cuisine is also rich in sweets and desserts. "Cozonac" is a traditional Easter bread filled with nuts and raisins, while "Papanasi" with sour cream and jam is a popular dessert often served on special occasions.

In recent years, Romanian cuisine has experienced a renaissance, with many restaurants in the larger cities offering a modern take on traditional dishes. This helps to promote and preserve the country's culinary identity, which reflects Romania's rich culture and history through its diversity and variety of flavors.

# Romanian wines and the wine regions

Romania has a long winemaking tradition that dates back to Roman times. The country's vineyards are spread over different regions and benefit from a temperate continental climate with fertile soils suitable for growing a variety of grape varieties. The main wine regions are mainly concentrated in Transylvania, Moldova, Muntenia, Dobruja, and Oltenia, with each region offering its own unique conditions and distinctive wine styles.

In Transylvania, vineyards are often nestled in hilly landscapes that benefit from cooler temperatures and a longer ripening period. Well-known grape varieties from this region include Fetească Albă, Fetească Neagră and Burgundy, which produce complex wines with fruity aromas and a balanced acid structure.

The Moldova region, also known as Moldova, is one of the largest and most important wine regions in Romania. Here, the soils are rich in minerals and the climate is ideal for the cultivation of grape varieties such as Grasa de Cotnari, Riesling, Sauvignon Blanc and Cabernet Sauvignon. The region is particularly known for its sweet white wines such as Cotnari and its fruity red wines, which are recognized both nationally and internationally.

Muntenia, with the capital Bucharest, is also an important wine-growing region, which is best known for its red wines. Grape varieties such as Merlot, Cabernet Sauvignon and Pinot Noir thrive particularly well here, with the proximity to the Danube and the temperate climate providing favourable conditions for viticulture.

Dobruja, located in the south-east of Romania, is known for its vineyards that stretch along the Black Sea coast. The region benefits from a temperate maritime climate and a variety of soils that allow the cultivation of grape varieties such as Chardonnay, Pinot Grigio and Muscat Ottonel. The wines from Dobruja are often characterized by their freshness and minerality.

Oltenia, located in the southwest of Romania, is an up-and-coming wine region characterized by its diversity of soils and microclimates. Both traditional Romanian grape varieties and international varieties such as Cabernet Franc, Syrah and Viognier are grown here, with winemakers focusing on quality and sustainability.

Overall, Romania offers a rich range of wines, ranging from vibrant whites to fruity rosés and complex reds. The country's wine industry has evolved a lot over the past few decades, with the introduction of modern techniques and sustainable practices to strengthen the quality and reputation of Romanian wines in the international market.

## The flora and fauna of Romania

Romania is home to a remarkable diversity of flora and fauna, which is characterized by its different landscapes and ecosystems. The geographical location between the temperate zone and the Balkan Peninsula contributes to this diversity, with both continental and Mediterranean elements present in nature.

The Romanian flora includes a wide variety of plant species, ranging from the Carpathians to the Danube Delta region to the plains and hills of Transylvania. In the Carpathians, there are extensive forests of beech, spruce and pine trees, which have been preserved as primeval forests and play an important role in the ecosystem. The Danube Delta Marshes are home to rare aquatic plants such as the yellow water lily and the water hyacinth, which support the delta's rich ecosystem.

Romania's wildlife is equally diverse, including a range of mammals, birds, reptiles, and amphibians. The country's largest mammals include brown bears, wolves, lynxes and red deer, which are native to the remote mountainous regions and forests of the Carpathians. Romania is also known for its rich bird diversity, especially in the Danube Delta, where more than 300 species of birds are found, including pelicans, cormorants, herons and various species of ducks.

The Danube Delta is a UNESCO World Heritage Site and one of Europe's most important wetlands, playing a key role in international bird migration and providing a refuge for endangered species such as the Caspian seal. Amphibians and reptiles are also present in Romania, with species such as the European pond turtle and fire salamander found in the country's humid forests and swamps.

In recent decades, Romania has taken measures to protect and preserve its natural habitats. National parks such as Retezat National Park and Semenic-Cheile-Carașului National Park serve as protected areas for native wildlife and offer opportunities for ecotourism and nature-related activities.

However, environmental challenges remain as agriculture, mining, and urbanization continue to put pressure on natural resources. Nevertheless, Romania remains an important center of biodiversity in Europe, making remarkable efforts to preserve and protect its unique ecosystems.

# Nature reserves and national parks

Romania has an impressive variety of nature reserves and national parks that serve to protect the country's rich biodiversity and natural ecosystems. These protected areas span different regions of the country and provide habitat for a wide variety of plant and animal species, some of which are threatened or rare.

One of the most famous national parks is the Retezat National Park in the Southern Carpathians, which was established in 1935 and is one of the oldest protected areas in Romania. The park encompasses a variety of landscapes, including alpine meadows, mountain lakes, and glacial lakes, overlooked by peaks such as Peleaga (2,509 m). It is home to a variety of animals, including bears, lynxes, deer and golden eagles, as well as rare plant species such as the edelweiss flower.

The Danube Delta, which has been a UNESCO World Heritage Site since 1991, is home to one of the largest wetlands in Europe. The delta encompasses a variety of habitats, including freshwater lakes, canals, reed beds, and salt marshes, which play an important role as a refuge for birds that rest during their migration between Africa and Europe. It is home to over 300 species of birds, including pelicans, cormorants, herons and various species of ducks, as well as rare mammals such as the Caspian seal.

Semenic-Cheile-Carașului National Park in the Southwest Carpathians is known for its spectacular gorges and waterfalls. The park provides habitat for a variety of wildlife, including wildcats, badgers, and chamois, as well as rare plant species that thrive in the rocky gorges.

Other important nature reserves are the Cozia National Park in the Southern Carpathians, the Ceahlău National Park in the Eastern Carpathians and the Iron Gates National Park on the Danube in the southwest of the country. Each of these areas plays an important role in the protection of native biodiversity, while also offering visitors the opportunity to experience and enjoy Romania's unspoiled nature.

The Romanian government and various environmental organizations are actively committed to the protection and sustainable development of these nature reserves. Through measures such as limiting human activities, promoting ecotourism and monitoring wildlife populations, they are helping to preserve these unique ecosystems for future generations.

# The Carpathians: Natural Wonders and Outdoor Adventure

The Carpathians extend over a length of about 1,500 kilometers and are the largest mountain system in Europe outside the Alpine arc. They pass through seven countries, including Romania, where they dominate much of the country in the center and north. These majestic mountains are not only a significant geographical feature of Romania, but also a center for natural beauty and outdoor activities.

The Romanian Carpathians are roughly divided into three main groups: the Eastern Carpathians, the Southern Carpathians and the Western Carpathians. Each of these regions has its own characteristic landscapes and ecosystems. The Eastern Carpathians, also known as the Forest Carpathians, are characterized by dense forests, deep valleys, and abundant wildlife. Here you will find rare animal species such as bears, lynxes and wolves, as well as a variety of bird species that live in the pristine forests and mountain ranges.

The Southern Carpathians are famous for their alpine landscapes, crystal clear mountain lakes and spectacular gorges. The Retezat National Park and the Făgăraș mountain range are among the highlights of this region, offering hikers and mountaineers a variety of routes and challenges. The highest peaks in Romania, such as Moldoveanu (2,544 m) and Vistea Mare (2,527 m), are located in the Southern Carpathians and attract outdoor enthusiasts from all over the world.

The Western Carpathians, also known as the Apuseni Mountains, are less alpine, but still impressive with their rolling hills, karst caves, and underground rivers. This region is also known for its traditional agriculture and picturesque villages that blend harmoniously with the natural surroundings.

The Carpathians offer a wealth of outdoor activities for adventurers of all kinds. From hiking and trekking to rock climbing, mountain biking and white water rafting, there are countless opportunities to explore the unspoiled nature and spectacular scenery. In winter, the Carpathians turn into a paradise for skiers and snowboarders, with ski resorts such as Poiana Brașov, Sinaia, and Bâlea Lake offering world-class slopes and breathtaking views.

The Carpathians are not only a retreat for outdoor enthusiasts, but also an important home for a variety of plant and animal species that thrive in the various habitats of the mountains. The protection of these natural resources is crucial for the preservation of biodiversity and the balance of ecosystems in this unique and fascinating region of Romania.

## The Danube and its importance for Romania

The Danube is the second longest river in Europe and one of the most important waterways on the continent. For Romania, the Danube is not only a geographical border in the west, but also an important source of economic, cultural and ecological resources. With a total length of about 2,860 kilometers, the Danube rises in the Black Forest in Germany and flows through ten countries, including Austria, Slovakia, Hungary, Croatia, Serbia, Bulgaria and finally Romania, before flowing into the Black Sea.

The Romanian section of the Danube stretches for about 1,075 kilometers and crosses the country from northwest to southeast. The river plays a central role in trade and transport, as it is an important waterway that provides access to the Black Sea. The Danube connects Romania with other European countries and facilitates trade in goods such as grain, petroleum products, metals and timber.

Ecologically, the Danube is of great importance to Romania, as it supports a variety of habitats and serves as a lifeline for a rich diversity of plant and animal species. The Danube Delta, the largest wetland in Europe, is a UNESCO World Heritage Site and a haven for hundreds of bird species, including rare species such as the Caspian seal. The delta also provides habitat for fish such as sturgeon, which is of economic importance for regional fisheries.

Historically, the Danube has played an important role in the development of Romania. It was an important trade route during the Roman period and the Middle Ages, when it was known as "Stradață". The cities along the Danube, such as Galați, Brăila and Tulcea, have developed into important commercial and cultural cities that have retained their importance as economic centers to this day.

The Danube is also a symbol of cultural diversity and connection. Along its shores are numerous historical sites, castles and monasteries that reflect the rich history and heritage of the region. The Danube is the subject of literature, art and music and has inspired numerous artists and writers.

Overall, the Danube remains a vital water artery for Romania, offering economic opportunities as well as preserving ecological diversity and cultural heritage. Their influence on the development of the country and their importance as a natural wonder and historical heritage are undisputed and shape the image and identity of Romania to this day.

# The Black Sea coast and its seaside resorts

The Black Sea coast of Romania stretches for about 245 kilometers along the eastern border of the country and offers a variety of seaside resorts and tourist attractions. The mild climate, golden sandy beaches and clear waters make this region a popular destination for recreation seekers and sun worshippers from all over Europe.

Mamaia is one of the most famous seaside resorts on the Romanian Black Sea coast and is located near the city of Constanța. It is famous for its long sandy beaches, modern hotels and lively seafront promenade. Mamaia attracts both families and partygoers who enjoy the variety of restaurants, bars and clubs along the coast. The beach is well equipped with sun loungers, umbrellas and water sports such as jet skiing and parasailing.

Also close to Constanța is the seaside resort of Eforie Nord, known for its healing maritime climate. There are several spa hotels and sanatoriums here that specialize in the treatment of respiratory diseases and rheumatic complaints. The beach of Eforie Nord stretches for several kilometers and offers peace and relaxation away from the hustle and bustle. Further south is the seaside resort of Neptun-

Olimp, known for its green parks and wooded areas that reach down to the beach. Ideal for nature lovers, these resorts offer a quieter atmosphere as well as plenty of opportunities for hiking and exploring the surrounding nature. The beach of Neptun-Olimp is wide and clean, ideal for families with children and for those looking for peace and relaxation. The Black Sea coast of Romania offers not only sun and beach, but also cultural sights and historical sites. Constanța, the largest city on the Black Sea coast, is a major port city with a rich history dating back to Roman times. Here, visitors can explore the Archaeological Museum, the Roman mosaic collection, and the historic city center.

For nature lovers, the northern part of the Black Sea coast offers the Danube Delta Biosphere Reserve, which covers 5,800 square kilometers and is one of the most important wetlands in Europe. The Danube Delta is home to a variety of animal species, including rare birds, fish, and plants, and offers opportunities for boat trips, bird watching, and ecotourism activities.

Overall, the Black Sea coast of Romania is a versatile and attractive holiday destination that attracts both those seeking relaxation and adventure seekers. With its picturesque beaches, rich history, and cultural heritage, it offers visitors an unforgettable experience on the Black Sea coast.

# Bucharest: capital between tradition and modernity

Bucharest, the capital of Romania, is a fascinating interplay of historical roots and modern life. As the largest city in the country and an important cultural, economic and political centre, it reflects Romania's multi-layered history and development.

The city was founded in the 15th century and has developed a rich cultural and architectural heritage over the centuries. Historic buildings such as the Palace of the Patriarchs, the Curtea Veche (Old Court) and the churches of the old town bear witness to Bucharest's former importance as the religious and political center of Wallachia. In the 19th century, the city experienced a renaissance under Prince Alexandru Ioan Cuza and later under King Carol I, which was characterized by intensive modernization and urban expansion.

Bucharest's architecture is a fascinating mix of different styles, including Romanian Renaissance, Neoclassicism, Art Nouveau, and Communist-era buildings. The wide boulevards, which were laid out during the reign of Nicolae Ceaușescu, symbolize the ambitious modernization plans of the communist regime and contrast with the picturesque little streets of the old town, where traditional cafes, restaurants and shops dominate the picture.

A highlight of the architectural splendor is undoubtedly the Palace of Parliament, a monument of the communist era that is considered the second largest building in the world after the Pentagon. With its 1,100 rooms and an area of over 365,000 square meters, the palace is symbolic of the power and megalomania of the Ceaușescu regime, but also of the architectural and cultural complexity of the city.

Today, Bucharest is a dynamic center of art, culture, and business in Southeastern Europe. The city is home to numerous museums, galleries, and cultural institutions such as the National Museum of Art, the Athenaeum, and the Village Museum, which attract visitors from all over the world. Bucharest is also known for its vibrant nightlife, music scene, and traditional cuisine, which reflects a variety of influences from the Balkan region.

Bucharest's population is a mix of different ethnic groups that contribute to the cultural diversity of the city. People are proud of their traditions and customs, which are celebrated at festivals, markets, and cultural events.

Romanian is the official language, but many residents also speak English, French or other European languages.

Economically, Bucharest plays a central role in Romania's economy. As a leading centre for finance, industry and services, the city attracts both national and international companies. The modern infrastructure, which provides well-developed transport links, supports economic development and contributes to the attractiveness of the city as an investment destination.

Overall, Bucharest embodies the beating heart of Romania, where tradition and modernity coexist harmoniously. The city is a source of inspiration for artists, writers, and visitors who want to experience its rich history, diverse culture, and dynamic energy.

# Timișoara: Capital of Culture and Multicultural Centre

Timișoara, located in the western part of Romania, is a city of cultural significance and multicultural diversity. It is the largest city in the Banat region and has a rich history dating back to Roman times. The city was first mentioned in a document in the 12th century and has been a melting pot of different cultures, ethnicities and religions over the centuries.

One of the most distinctive features of Timișoara is its architecture, which is shaped by different eras. The old town, also called Cetate, is a lively center with Baroque, Neoclassical and Art Nouveau buildings. The main square (Piața Victoriei) is characterized by magnificent buildings such as the Orthodox Cathedral, the Serbian Orthodox Cathedral and the Catholic Cathedral, which reflect the religious diversity of the city.

In the 18th and 19th centuries, Timișoara became a significant cultural and economic center, inhabited by various ethnic groups such as Romanians, Germans, Serbs, Hungarians, and Jews. This led to a thriving cultural scene, which is still visible today in the form of theatres, opera houses, museums and galleries. The National Opera and Ballet House, the Banat German State Theatre and the Museum of Banat Farmhouses are just a few examples of the city's cultural institutions.

Timișoara is also known as the "City of the Revolution" as it played a central role in the Romanian uprising of 1989, which led to the fall of the communist regime of Nicolae Ceaușescu. The revolution began in Timișoara and quickly spread to other cities in the country, contributing to the restoration of democracy and the modernization of Romania.

The city is proud of its multicultural identity and celebrates this with various festivals and events. The Timișoara Music Festival, the JazzTM Festival and the International Theatre Festival are just some of the events that express the cultural diversity of the city. Timișoara was named the European Capital of Culture in 2021, further underlining its importance as the cultural center of Europe.

Today, Timișoara is an important center for education, research and technology in Romania. West University and Polytechnic University are prestigious educational institutions that attract students from home and abroad. The city also has a growing economy, especially in the automotive industry, information technology, and services, resulting in dynamic development and steady population growth.

Overall, Timișoara embodies the harmonious coexistence of tradition and modernity, of history and innovation. The city remains a magnet for visitors who want to experience its cultural diversity, rich history, and vibrant atmosphere.

## Cluj-Napoca: university city and cultural hub

Cluj-Napoca, also known as Cluj-Napoca, is a significant city in northwestern Romania and the largest city in the Transylvania region. With a rich history dating back to Roman times, Cluj-Napoca is now a dynamic university city and a cultural hub that attracts visitors from all over the world.

The city was founded by the Romans in the 2nd century AD and was then called "Napoca". Later, in the Middle Ages, it became an important trading centre in the Hungarian kingdom under the name "Kolozsvár". After the First World War, it became part of Romania and was given the name Cluj-Napoca, the name "Cluj" being derived from the Latin "Clusium", which means "closed".

A central aspect of Cluj-Napoca is its role as an educational center. Babeș-Bolyai University, one of the oldest and most prestigious universities in Romania, is based here and attracts students from home and abroad. Known for its faculties in the humanities, science, medicine, and engineering, the university contributes significantly to the intellectual life of the city.

Culturally, Cluj-Napoca offers a variety of sights and cultural institutions. The Ethnographic Museum of Transylvania, the Museum of Art and the Museum of the History of Pharmacy are just a few examples of the museums that reflect the rich history and culture of the region. The city is also known for its historic churches and cathedrals, including the Gothic St. Michael's Church and the Baroque Franciscan Church.

Cluj-Napoca is a city of festivals and cultural events. The Transilvania International Film Festival (TIFF) is one of the largest film festivals in Central and Eastern Europe and attracts filmmakers and cineastes from all over the world every year. Untold Festival, one of Romania's largest music festivals, is also held in Cluj-Napoca and features a variety of musical genres and artists.

Economically, Cluj-Napoca is an important center for technology and innovation in Romania. The city is home to numerous IT companies and start-ups that benefit from the well-educated workforce of university graduates. The industry is closely linked to Babeș-Bolyai University and the Technical University, which drive research and development in various fields such as computer science, biotechnology and electronics.

The population of Cluj-Napoca is diverse and multicultural, with a mix of Romanians, Hungarians, Germans, and other ethnic groups. The city prides itself on its cultural diversity and celebrates this through traditional festivals and events that take place throughout the year. The languages spoken in the city are Romanian, Hungarian, and German, reflecting the historical and cultural ties with the various communities in the region.

Overall, Cluj-Napoca embodies the combination of tradition and modernity, of history and innovation. The city remains a major draw for visitors and residents who want to experience its diverse culture, rich history, and vibrant atmosphere.

# Sibiu: European Capital of Culture and Historical Heritage

Sibiu, also known as Sibiu, is a city in the Transylvania region in central Romania. It was founded by German settlers in the 12th century and was an important trading center in Transylvania for a long time. The city is picturesquely located in the middle of the southern Carpathians and is known for its well-preserved medieval architecture.

Throughout its history, Sibiu has been an important center of German culture and trade in eastern Central Europe. The city was a member of the Hanseatic League and an important economic and cultural center in the Kingdom of Hungary. The German population contributed significantly to the development of the city, which is still reflected today in the architecture, traditions and customs.

A highlight of architecture in Sibiu is the old town, which is characterized by narrow streets, Gothic and Baroque buildings, and historic churches. The Great and Small Ring Roads (Piața Mare and Piața Mică) are centrally located squares surrounded by magnificent bourgeois houses with colourful facades and ornate bay windows. The

Protestant parish church and the Catholic Trinity Church are outstanding examples of sacred architecture from different eras.

Sibiu was named the European Capital of Culture in 2007, which underlines its cultural importance in Europe. The city is home to numerous cultural institutions, including the Brukenthal Museum, the oldest museum in Romania, which exhibits an impressive collection of European art. The ASTRA National Museum of Outdoor Folklore showcases traditional rural life in Romania with over 400 historic buildings and farms.

In addition to its rich history and architecture, Sibiu is also a center for festivals and cultural events. The Sibiu International Theatre Festival, which was launched in 1993, attracts renowned theatre companies from all over the world every year and is considered one of the most important theatre festivals in Eastern Europe. The February Festival and the Jazz & More Festival are other cultural highlights that take place throughout the year.

Economically, Sibiu plays an important role in Romania, especially in the automotive industry and manufacturing. The city is home to plants of large multinational companies such as Continental and ThyssenKrupp, which contribute to the economic development of the region. The well-educated population and central location in Romania make Sibiu an attractive location for investment and business activities.

The population of Sibiu is diverse, with a mix of Romanians, Hungarians, Germans and other ethnic groups. The city prides itself on its cultural diversity and promotes intercultural dialogue through various programs and initiatives. The official languages are Romanian and German, reflecting the historical and cultural ties with the different communities in the region.

Overall, Sibiu embodies the combination of historical heritage and European Capital of Culture, of tradition and modernity. The city remains a significant cultural and economic center in Romania and a magnetic draw for visitors who want to experience its rich history, architecture, and cultural diversity.

# Brasov: Gateway to the Carpathians and medieval flair

Brasov, also known as Brasov, is one of the most important cities in the Transylvania region in the central part of Romania. The city is picturesquely nestled between the Southern Carpathians and is known for its well-preserved medieval architecture, which has been shaped by various European cultures.

Founded in the 13th century by German settlers, Brasov was for a long time an important trading point on the trade route between Eastern and Western Europe. The German influences are still visible today in the architecture of the old town, with its colorful houses, Gothic churches and the mighty defensive towers that once protected the city.

The old town of Brasov is dominated by the Town Hall Tower, a symbol of the city that was once part of the city's fortifications. The Market Square (Piața Sfatului) is a lively center with cafes, restaurants and historic buildings. The Black Church, an impressive 14th-century Gothic cathedral, is one of the city's outstanding religious structures and is home to one of the largest organs in Europe.

In addition to medieval architecture, Brasov also offers a variety of cultural sights. The Brasov County History Museum presents artifacts and exhibits related to the history of the region from ancient times to the present day. The First Romanian School, the oldest Romanian school in Transylvania, showcases the historical heritage of Romania's educational tradition.

The city is also a popular destination for outdoor enthusiasts who want to explore the surrounding nature of the Carpathian Mountains. Nearby Mount Tampa offers hiking trails and spectacular views over the city and surrounding valleys. In winter, the nearby Poiana Brașov ski resort attracts winter sports enthusiasts from all over Europe.

Brasov is an important economic and cultural hub in Romania. The city is a center for tourism, trade and services and is home to companies from various industries. The proximity to Bucharest's Henri Coandă International Airport and good transport links make Brasov an attractive location for investment and business development.

Brasov's population is diverse and multicultural, with a mix of Romanians,

Hungarians, Germans, and other ethnic groups. The city celebrates its cultural diversity through festivals and events that take place throughout the year. The Brasov International Film Festival & Market and the Cerbul de Aur (Golden Deer Festival) are just a few examples of cultural highlights that attract visitors.

Overall, Brasov embodies the combination of historical heritage and natural beauty, of tradition and modernity. The city remains a magnet for visitors who want to experience its rich history, architecture, and charming ambience of the Carpathian Mountains.

## Iași: Cultural and intellectual stronghold of the East

Iași, the former capital of Romania and the largest city in the historic region of Moldova, is considered a cultural and intellectual stronghold of the East. The city, founded in the 14th century, is rich in history and traditions that are still maintained today.

Culturally, Iași is known for its significant educational institutions, including Alexandru Ioan Cuza University, the oldest university in Romania, founded in 1860. This university has a long tradition of excellence in the humanities and natural sciences and attracts students from all over the country.

The city is also a center of Romanian literature and art. Iași has been home to many important writers and artists, including Mihai Eminescu, who is considered the national poet of Romania. The literary and art scene is dominated by the Museum of Romanian Literature and the Vasile Alecsandri National Theatre, which offers a wide range of plays and cultural events.

Architecturally, Iași impresses with its well-preserved old town, which offers a mixture of Romanian, Byzantine and Gothic architecture. The Palace of Culture (Palatul Culturii), a landmark of the city, is home to the Moldavian History Museum, which showcases art galleries and an impressive collection of historical artifacts. The three Orthodox churches - the Metropolitan Cathedral, the Trei Ierarhi Church and the Golia Monastery - are significant religious structures that reflect the religious and cultural identity of the city.

Iași is also known for its diverse cultural scene, enriched by festivals and cultural events. The International Theatre Festival in Iași, which takes place annually, attracts theatre companies from all over the world and provides a platform for artistic exchange and innovation. The International Festival of Literature and Translation (FILIT) is another outstanding event that brings together authors and literature lovers to celebrate the diversity of literature.

Economically, Iași plays an important role in the Romanian economy, especially in the field of IT and technology. The city is a significant center for IT companies and outsourcing services, which contributes to strong growth and positive economic development. The well-educated workforce and modern infrastructure make Iași an attractive location for international investment.

The population of Iași is diverse and multicultural, with a mix of Romanians, Moldovans, Hungarians and other ethnic groups. The city promotes cultural diversity and intercultural dialogue through various programs and initiatives to promote cultural heritage and shared values.

Overall, Iași embodies Romania's rich cultural and intellectual tradition and remains a major center for education, art, and innovation in the eastern part of the country.

# Constanta: Port City and Ancient Past

Constanta, a major port city on Romania's Black Sea coast, has a rich history that dates back to ancient times. Originally founded by the Greeks as Tomis, Constanta was an important trading post and an important city of the Roman Empire. The city is strategically located at the mouth of the Danube River and has experienced a variety of cultural influences over the centuries.

Constanta's ancient past is still visible today in its archaeological remains, including Roman monuments such as the Ovid Monument, dedicated to the Roman poet Ovid, who lived here in exile. The Archaeological Museum displays an impressive collection of artifacts from the Roman period and other historical periods.

In the Middle Ages, Constanta was ruled by the Byzantines and later by the Genoese and Turks, before finally becoming part of the Romanian state. The city experienced a significant economic and cultural heyday in the 19th century during the reign of the Romanian kings.

Today, Constanta is an important economic center in Romania, especially in the area of seaport and shipping. The port of Constanta is the largest Black Sea port and plays an important role in trade and tourism. The city is a popular destination for cruises and combines modern port infrastructures with historic charm.

The architecture of Constanta reflects the diverse cultural influences, from the Roman remains to the Ottoman buildings. The city centre is characterised by elegant Art Nouveau buildings and historic churches, including the Orthodox Cathedral of Constanta.

The population of Constanta is diverse and multicultural, with a mix of Romanians, Turks, Tatars and other ethnic groups. The city celebrates its cultural diversity through various festivals and events, including the Constanta Maritime Festival, which honors the city's maritime tradition.

Constanta is also known for its beautiful beaches and resorts along the Black Sea coast. Mamaia, a popular seaside resort near Constanta, attracts thousands of tourists every year who enjoy the sunny beaches and lively nightlife.

Overall, Constanta embodies the combination of ancient past and modern present, of historical heritage and maritime dynamism. The city remains an important hub for trade, culture and tourism in the eastern part of Europe.

# The Moldavian Monasteries: UNESCO World Heritage Sites and Spiritual Oases

The Moldavian monasteries, also known as the Moldavian churches, form a remarkable group of churches and monasteries in the Moldova region of Romania. These architectural masterpieces are famous for their painted churches, ornate facades, and historical significance as spiritual centers and places of worship.

The Moldavian monasteries were built between the 15th and 16th centuries during the reign of the Moldavian princes. They were not only religious sites, but also served as centers of cultural and artistic development. The monasteries were often built in remote locations in the middle of a picturesque landscape, surrounded by dense forests and high mountains, which added to their special atmosphere.

The most famous Moldavian monasteries have been included in the UNESCO World Heritage List, including the Voroneț Monastery, the Sucevița Monastery, the Moldovița Monastery, the Humor Monastery and the Arbore Monastery. Each of these monasteries is known for its unique architecture and magnificent frescoes depicting biblical scenes, legends of saints, and symbolic motifs. The Voroneț Monastery, known as the "Sistine Chapel of the East", is famous for its vibrant blue colors used in the frescoes, especially the "Last Judgement". The Sucevița Monastery is known for its green color and extensive fresco cycles depicting the life of Christ and the saints.

The frescoes of the Moldavian monasteries are not only artistically valuable, but also of great historical and religious importance. They are testimonies to the Orthodox beliefs and spiritual values that have shaped Moldovan society. The paintings were not only intended for the faithful, but also for the education and instruction of the people about the Christian doctrine. The monasteries also played an important role as cultural centers, where manuscripts were copied, books were written, and handicrafts were developed. The monks who lived in the monasteries were often also artists and craftsmen who contributed to the development of Romanian art and culture.

Today, the Moldavian monasteries are not only important religious sites, but also tourist attractions that attract visitors from all over the world. They are symbols of Romanian history, culture and spirituality and stand for the connection of faith, art and nature in a unique and unmistakable way.

# Transylvania: myths, legends and historical castles

Transylvania, the historical region in the center of Romania, is famous for its rich cultural and natural diversity, as well as for the numerous myths and legends that surround it. Nestled between the Carpathian Mountains in the east and Transylvania in the west, Transylvania stretches over a picturesque landscape of rolling hills, dense forests and fertile valleys.

The region is closely linked to the history of the Transylvanian Saxons, the Hungarian and Romanian populations who lived here for centuries. Transylvania has been a melting pot of different cultures and ethnicities, which has resulted in a unique cultural diversity.

One of the most famous associations with Transylvania is the legend of Count Dracula, which is based on the historical background of the Wallachian prince Vlad III, who was known as "Vlad Drăculea". Its birthplace, Sighișoara, is a well-preserved medieval town and a popular tourist destination.

In addition to the legends, Transylvania is known for its impressive historic castles and fortresses, often built on hills or in strategic positions to dominate the landscape. One of the most famous castles is Bran Castle, which is often mistakenly associated with the Dracula legend, but is actually an impressive example of medieval architecture.

Another notable castle is Hunyadi Castle in Hunedoara, also known as Corvin Castle, which is considered one of the largest and most imposing Gothic castles in Eastern Europe. It is a symbol of Hungarian history and architecture in Romania.

The historical and cultural diversity of Transylvania is also reflected in its cities, such as Cluj-Napoca, Sibiu and Braşov. These cities are not only rich in history, but also centers for art, culture, and education.

Transylvania's natural beauty is complemented by its numerous national parks and nature reserves, including Apuseni National Park and the Rodna Mountain Range. These areas offer hikers and nature lovers a variety of outdoor activities, including hiking, mountaineering, and wildlife viewing.

Overall, Transylvania is a region of fascinating beauty and cultural significance, attracting visitors from all over the world, attracted by its legends, historic castles, and a landscape that is both wild and picturesque. It remains one of the most unique and charming regions in Europe, whose wealth of history and nature delights every visitor.

# Transylvania: Multicultural Diversity and Historical Traces

Transylvania, also known as Transylvania, is a historically and culturally rich region in the center of Romania. The region covers a diverse landscape of rolling hills, fertile valleys and imposing mountain ranges of the Carpathian Mountains. Named after the seven main castles that once protected the region, Transylvania is a symbol of multicultural diversity and historical significance.

The history of Transylvania is closely linked to the various ethnicities and cultures that have settled here over the centuries. The Transylvanian Saxons, a German ethnic group, played an important role in the economy and cultural development of the region. Their traces can still be seen today in the well-preserved cities such as Sibiu, Brașov and Sighișoara, all of which are UNESCO World Heritage Sites.

In addition to the Transylvanian Saxons, Hungarian and Romanian communities have also shaped the history and culture of Transylvania. This cultural diversity is evident in the architecture of the cities, festivals and customs, as well as in the language and traditional cuisine of the region.

Historically, Transylvania has been a centre of trade and culture, as evidenced by the numerous medieval castles, churches and fortifications. Bran Castle, often mistakenly associated with the Dracula legend, is an example of the imposing architecture built to defend the region.

In addition to its rich history, Transylvania is also known for its natural beauty. National parks such as Apuseni National Park offer hiking trails through karst landscapes and caves that are part of the region's unique geological formations.

The multicultural diversity and historical traces make Transylvania a fascinating destination for visitors interested in history, culture and nature. The region remains a symbol of tolerance and coexistence of different ethnic groups and religions, which have preserved their own identity and at the same time share a rich and dynamic common history.

## Bukovina: Artistic frescoes and traditional wooden churches

Bukovina, a historical region in northeastern Romania, is famous for its ornate frescoes and traditional wooden churches, which make up a significant part of the region's cultural heritage. Bukovina stretches over a picturesque landscape of green valleys, forested hills and gentle mountain ranges, nestled between the Eastern Carpathians and the Ukrainian Carpathians in the north.

One of Bucovina's most outstanding cultural attractions is the painted monasteries, especially the UNESCO World Heritage monasteries of Voroneț, Humor, Moldovița, Sucevița, and Arbore. These Orthodox monasteries date back to the 15th and 16th centuries and are known for their vibrant frescoes depicting biblical scenes, saints, and prophetic depictions in bold colors. The frescoes are not only religious works of art, but also historical testimonies to the Orthodox practice of faith and the cultural identity of the region.

In addition to the painted monasteries, the traditional wooden churches are another outstanding feature of Bucovina. These churches, often made of wood and built without nails, are known for their unique architecture and richly decorated iconostasis inside. The wooden churches are a living example of the region's traditional craftsmanship and religious culture.

Bukovina has historically been a melting pot of different cultures and ethnicities, including Romanians, Ukrainians, Germans, and Jews. This diversity is reflected in the architecture, customs and traditional music of the region. Bukovina was also a center of intellectual life, especially in the 19th and early 20th centuries, when the region became known for its literature, music, and art.

Today, Bukovina is a popular destination for visitors interested in history, art, and culture. In addition to the monasteries and wooden churches, the picturesque villages, thermal baths and the natural beauty of the Carpathians also attract hikers and nature lovers. Bukovina remains a symbol of the rich cultural heritage and spiritual significance in Romania and beyond.

# The Romanian language: origin, dialects and peculiarities

The Romanian language is one of the Eastern Romance languages and belongs to the Indo-European language family. It developed from the Vulgar Latin introduced by the Roman soldiers and settlers who settled in the ancient province of Dacia. This region, which includes present-day Romania, has experienced various cultural influences throughout history, which are reflected in the language.

A characteristic feature of the Romanian language is its close relationship with Italian, French, Spanish and Portuguese. These languages together form the Romance languages, which emerged from Latin. However, the Romanian language has also absorbed a large number of Slavic, Hungarian, Greek and Turkish loanwords, which distinguish it from other Romance languages.

There are different dialects of the Romanian language in Romania, which vary from region to region. The main dialects are the Wallachian dialect, the Moldavian dialect and the Banat dialect. These dialects differ mainly in pronunciation, grammar and vocabulary, with the Wallachian dialect being considered the standard dialect for the Romanian literary language.

The Romanian language uses the Latin alphabet, but it is extended by some special diacritics that mark the pronunciation and stress of the words. These diacritics are the Ă (A with breve), Â (A with circumflex), Î (I with circumflex), Ş (S with circumflex) and Ţ (T with circumflex). They are an integral part of Romanian spelling and contribute to the precision of pronunciation.

Due to its linguistic diversity and its connection to different cultures, the Romanian language is not only a means of communication, but also an essential part of Romania's national identity. Through them, traditions, customs and stories are preserved and passed on that reflect the rich history and cultural diversity of the country. The Romanian language thus remains a living expression of Romania's past and present.

# Travel tips and practical information

This chapter summarises important travel tips and practical information for travellers to Romania. Romania is a diverse travel destination with a rich history, fascinating culture and breathtaking landscapes that attract visitors from all over the world. Here you will find useful information on travel planning, entry and the most important sights of the country.

To enter Romania, most visitors from EU countries or from countries that are part of the Schengen area only need a valid passport or identity card. Visitors from other countries should check the current visa requirements before starting their trip. The local currency is the Romanian Leu (RON), and there are numerous ATMs and banks where you can exchange money.

The best time to visit Romania is usually in spring (April to June) and autumn (September to October), when the weather is pleasant and the landscape is in full bloom. In summer, temperatures can be high, especially in the cities, while winter can be cold and snowy, but this also means the ski season in the Carpathians.

Romania offers a variety of accommodation, from luxury hotels in the big cities to cozy guesthouses and farms in the countryside. It is advisable to book accommodation in advance, especially in high season and in popular destinations such as Bucharest, Brasov, Sibiu and Cluj-Napoca.

There are several options available for public transportation in Romania, including buses, trains, and trams in the cities, as well as regional buses and taxis. The road network is well developed, but driving conditions can be more challenging in remote areas.

Romania is known for its hospitality, and visitors are often warmly welcomed. Romanian cuisine is rich and varied, with traditional dishes such as sarmale (cabbage rolls), mămăligă (corn porridge) and various meat dishes. Local specialties and wines should definitely be tasted.

Important cultural attractions in Romania are the painted monasteries of Bucovina, the medieval castles and fortresses in Transylvania, and the historic towns and villages, which often offer well-preserved architecture and unique atmosphere.

For active vacationers and nature lovers, the Romanian Carpathians offer numerous hiking and outdoor activities, while the Black Sea coast with its beaches and seaside resorts attracts those seeking relaxation.

Overall, Romania offers a fascinating mix of history, culture, and nature that delights every visitor. With these travel tips and practical information, you can plan and enjoy your trip to Romania in the best possible way.

## Famous people from Romania

This chapter presents some of the most important personalities from Romania, whose influence spans various fields such as politics, literature, art, science and sports.

An outstanding name in Romanian history is Nicolae Ceaușescu, who served as the country's head of state from 1965 to 1989 and shaped a controversial political era. His authoritarian rule and attempts to make Romania more independent of the Soviet Union have attracted both national and international attention.

In the world of literature, Mircea Eliade, a renowned writer and religious scholar of the 20th century, stands out. Known for his works on religion and mythology, including "Maitreyi" and "The Pillar and the Corn", he shaped modern Romanian literature and enjoyed worldwide recognition.

George Enescu is considered one of the most important Romanian composers and violinists of the 20th century. His musical work includes symphonies, chamber music, operas and concerts, which are highly appreciated both in Romania and internationally.

In the field of athletes, Nadia Comăneci has made a name for herself as a legendary artistic gymnast. She was the first gymnast to score a perfect 10 at the 1976 Montreal Olympics and win multiple gold medals, making her an icon of international sport.

Henri Coandă, a pioneer in aviation, is known for his groundbreaking work in the field of aerodynamics and aircraft design. He developed the world's first jet aircraft, and the "Coandă effect" named after him is a fundamental concept in fluid mechanics.

The list of famous people from Romania also includes artists such as Constantin Brâncuși, one of the most important sculptors of the 20th century, known for his modernist sculptures, and Eugen Ionescu, an outstanding playwright and writer of the theater of the absurd.

In addition to these outstanding personalities, many other Romanians have made significant contributions in their respective fields and have left their mark on the country's cultural heritage. Their works and achievements are an integral part of Romania's rich and diverse history, which is also widely recognized internationally.

# Future prospects and challenges

Romania's future prospects and challenges face a dynamic tension of economic, political and social factors. While the country has made significant progress in areas such as economic development and infrastructure in recent years, there are still many challenges ahead.

A key issue is economic diversification and modernisation. Romania is striving to reduce its dependence on certain industrial sectors and to broaden its economy. In particular, the promotion of innovation and technology as well as the improvement of the education and skills of the workforce are crucial for future competitiveness.

Politically, Romania faces the challenge of strengthening democratic institutions and intensifying the fight against corruption. Although progress has been made, concerns remain about the rule of law and the independence of the judiciary, which affect the country's governance.

In the social sector, the demographic challenges are significant. A decline in the population and an ageing society pose major challenges for the social system. Promoting the birth rate and ensuring a sustainable pension policy are essential aspects for securing the future.

Environmental problems such as air and water pollution, as well as the conservation of natural resources and biodiversity, are also key concerns. The promotion of renewable energy and sustainable agricultural practices are at the heart of efforts to reduce environmental impact and ensure environmental sustainability.

At the international level, Romania aspires to play an active role in the European and global community. Participation in international organizations and the promotion of diplomatic relations are of strategic importance for the geopolitical positioning of the country and its economic integration into the global market.

Overall, Romania's future offers opportunities for growth and development, but at the same time poses challenges that need to be addressed with determination and smart governance in order to ensure long-term prosperity and stability.

## Closing remarks

The end of a book about Romania marks not only a conclusion, but also a beginning. It is a moment of reflection on the rich history, diverse culture and impressive nature of this fascinating country. Romania, located in the heart of Europe, uniquely combines influences from East and West, which are reflected in its architecture, cuisine and music.

From the majestic Carpathian Mountains to the rolling hills of the wine regions, the country offers a landscape of breathtaking beauty that enchants visitors and locals alike. The rich biodiversity and protected national parks testify to Romania's commitment to protecting the environment and preserving its natural resources.

The history of Romania, from the ancient Dacian cultures to Roman rule to the Ottoman occupation and later unification, is a history of change and resilience. The achievements of Romanian literature, music and art have gained worldwide recognition and contribute to Europe's cultural diversity.

Modern challenges such as economic transformation, demographic change and political stability pose significant tests for the country. Nevertheless, there is an undeniable sense of hope and progress that shapes Romania's future.

In the end, Romania remains a land of contrasts and opportunities, a place that welcomes its visitors with hospitality and enchants them with its beauty and cultural richness. May this book help to deepen the understanding and appreciation of Romania's rich heritage and open up new perspectives on its future.

Printed in Great Britain
by Amazon